The Long Way Home

Mary Charlton

BookLeaf Publishing

Presentation by *BookLeaf Publishing*

Web: www.bookleafpub.com

E-mail: info@bookleafpub.com

ISBN: 9789395756266

First edition 2022

Poetry

Poetry.
Where raw emotions and fresh feelings fill the pages,
Yet when asked to explain, only a tremor and a whimper can be formed upon my lips.
I can flood the pages with emotions, and quench the papered thirst
But unable to fill the hunger sought from a cherished one.

My inability to produce words unleashes nothing but anger in the form of venom,
Resulting in the ghastly taste upon my tongue
And here I am, oozing the ink from my pen.
My love, please don't grow weary of me.
I may not speak today, but maybe tomorrow.

The Broken Man

I've fooled around with the older man,
I've fooled around with the younger man,
I've fooled around with the married man
And I've fooled around with the single man.

I've danced with the gentlemen, and drank with
the pretty men.
I've travelled with the quiet man, and exchanged
secrets with the loud man.

I've kissed abusive men, I've rolled around with
the honest men.
I've had adventures with deceitful men and
broke the hearts of good men.

They may have set my sensations tingling, my
lips pulsing with excitement.
They may have had me roaring with laughter
and whispering sweet nothings,
They may have caused me pain and they may
have caused me happiness.

But none of them, ever, caught my soul on fire
and electrified my heart.
Like the broken man.

Recovery

Lying here, with the cold ceramic pressing
against my skin.
The drip... drip... drip.... of the tap,
The sounds of shouting reduce to a whisper
Drip
Drip
Drip.

A sound all too familiar.
But this time, there's no hot liquid running down
my arm
There's no pulsation from a wound,
There is no cold metal in between my fingers.

Drip
Drip
Drip.

The sharp sting is no longer throbbing,
And I, am no longer sobbing.
Watching the water ripple, with no tinge of
colour.

Drip
Drip

Drip.

Then silence. Peace. Quiet.

But the voices are still here, are yours?

A Gentle Reminder

5

If what we really want is to feel okay,
happy, loving and loved,
then death is not an option to achieve those.

Playing with Fire

Let's ignite this tender spark, we can't let it die
when it's just begun.
Gently does it now,
Don't let the cold wind blow.
In a soft combined effort, we'll have to cradle it.

My darling, we can sit and enjoy the warmth
that caresses our skin.
We can listen to the soothing sound of the
crackling,
Don't play with the fire, you'll get burnt but I'll
let the flames dance up my arm to protect you.
Here, let me guide you to the shade.

Do you share the burden, or watch me burn?

The Devils Chin

Like a young romantic, you called me baby.
You held my hands and hung on to every word I
exhaled,
My walls were down, no barrier to climb.
We waltzed right in, tumbling in with our eyes
and hands searching only for one another.
You led me on, high up on hope.
Presented me at the gates, crown glistening upon
my head.
You told me secrets and let me in, you promised
you'd be back; yet I'm still here waiting.
My dark haired prince, with the devils chin.
I should've known you'd be charming,
You kissed my hands and my soul sang.
We danced to the rhythm you played, was I
blinded by stupidity?
I fell into your arms, I breathed in your lies
The aroma poisoning my anguished mind.
Oh the handsome devil, struck again.

Demons

You tamed my demons then left me alone to pick
up the pieces,
Now they're louder than ever.
So loud, you can't hear my cries for help.

Poison

It's poison.
It's poison, seeping through our pores.
It's corroding our minds, our vision.

Are we really happy?
Happiness is to smile.
Are we just surviving?
Are we truly happy, what is happiness to you?

We drink poison, we digest venom, is it to numb
the ever growing pain? Does that make you
happy?

Does the burnt out cigarette lying on the floor;
that left a burnt crisp on your skin, does that
make you happy?
Does it make you feel free?

The ever growing masks change in society. The
many faces we fear, the faces we may become.

Where does it end?

Does it end in happiness? Does it end in desire?
Does it end in despair?

When, when does it end?

Into the Woods.

13 years since you took her from me.
13 years since the darkness took residency,
refusing to be evicted.
The glimpses of peace fleet through my mind as
I try to seize her.
Try to grasp with both hands, the harder I try, the
more she slips away.
Playfully slipping through my fingers.

Maybe I'm meant to be left with a deepening
hole,
A lost part of my soul.

Sand Castles.

A trip to the beach, feet in the sand.
I couldn't help but compare these tiny little rocks
to the avalanche of my mind.
Sand castles, they require time, effort and
patience; yet takes the tiniest of blows for it to
crumble.
Each one representing the fragile state of mind.
I progress on to another, the first is already in the
state of decay.
As I final one is finally erected, the originals are
scarcely there.
The harder you grip, the more it slips through
your fingers.
But however fragile the sand may be, it's always
ready to be rebuilt until it is left in it's peaceful,
beautiful original state.

Numb.

I don't know the shade grey.
I'm either black or white,
I'm all or nothing.
My mind is either buzzing with everything,
Or floating around in nothingness.

Cravings

What do you do on a day like today,
When all you want is to hang your head,
Leave your lungs full of smoke and let the taste
of vodka linger on your tongue?
When the burning sensations pulsates on your
skin, and your veins look full of blood longing
for its release,
What do you do on a day like today?

Dreams Don't Come True

My heart is deaf and completely blinded at the
beauty before it,
The concoction of happiness and scepticism is
overwhelming.
Maybe just enjoy it and savour it whilst it lasts,
Maybe prepare for heartbreak and accept happy
endings are just for fairy tales.

The Beauty Within

You're a shining diamond amongst the blackened
coal,
You radiate beauty and love through a broken
shell, you shine so brightly.
I'm in awe of you.
Your silent courage speaks a thousand words,
which render me speechless.
I am in awe, of such a beautiful soul.

I Found You

You make love easy, like it only exists to us.
Our own special song.
Everything has been worth it, just to fall into
your arms.
As we sway to our own melody, I'm glad I
finally found you.
You make love easy.

Safe

I'd absorb all your pain and heartache, just to save you from the hurt.
Wrap you up and keep you safe, if it meant you were carefree.
I'd make your pain my own, so it could never make its way back to you again.

Relapse

I am my own worst enemy,
In many ways I've perfected the art of creating
scenarios in my head;
And let them wreck havoc in my safe haven.

They dance with the devil and drink with my
demons.
The Angels can't enter this treacherous hole,
So here I lay in silence, ignoring the whispers
that encourage my cravings.
I'll wait in the dark, till the light appears again.

Forever Yours

My darling, you'll forever live on these pages.
You made a poet fall in love.

Do I Write Love Poems Correctly?

Overcome with emotions I've never felt before,
How I hope they are here to stay.
I thank you for making me feel something,
anything other than being numb.
You saved me, without even realising.
You'll always be my hero,
Oh, you are so brave in so many ways.

To My Solider, My Soulmate.

My promise to you is to never let you down
Even though it'll pain me to watch you leave, I
promise to be here to say goodbye.
While you're away, wherever you may be
I promise to be here waiting for your return.
I'll think about you daily, until I'm in your arms
again.
I promise to stay loyal to you, for I know no
matter where life takes me
It'll never take me from you, for we are always
under the same stars.
I promise to love you to the moon and back
forever and always.

www.ingramcontent.com/pod-product-compliance
Lightning Source LLC
La Vergne TN
LVHW010023200726
843495LV00015B/1907